PRAYERS

of

Renewal

Contributing Writers

Nancy Parker Brummett

Lain Ehmann

Marie D. Jones

Publications International, Ltd.

Cover Photo: Shutterstock

Contributing Writers

Nancy Parker Brummett is a freelance writer, columnist, and the author of four books who lives in Colorado Springs, CO. Leading women closer to the heart of God is the hallmark of her speaking and writing ministries. To learn more about her life and work, visit www.nancyparkerbrummett.com.

Lain Ehmann is a Massachusetts-based writer and mom to three.

Marie D. Jones is the author of several best-selling nonfiction books and a contributing author to numerous inspirational books, including *Echoes of Love: Sisters, Mother, Grandmother, Friends, Graduation, Wedding; Mother's Daily Prayer Book;* and *When You Lose Someone You Love: God Will Comfort You.* She can be reached at www.mariedjones.com.

Acknowledgments

Scripture quotations are taken from the *New Revised Standard Version* of the Bible. Copyright © 1989 by the Division of Christian Education of the National Council of the Churches of Christ in the United States of America. Used by permission. All rights reserved.

GOD RENEWS

A life and a spirit can become stale with the stresses and challenges of being, doing, and achieving. In God we find an opportunity for a new start, any time we need it. In faith, we can ask for the grace of a renewed spirit that sees the world through new eyes, with the same awe and wonder we had as children.

New jobs, a new spouse, new things may make us temporarily feel better, but then we are back again feeling a sense of emptiness and uselessness. That is because only God can bring us to the brink of a new life, with newfound strength, courage, and trust that life can be joyful and filled with light and love. The renewal of the one who loves us most is like no other, laying before us an unwalked path that is ours and ours alone, but one we won't have to walk alone.

When we feel old, God can make us feel young at heart. When we feel tired, God can make us feel as sprightly as a newborn colt running through tall grass. When we feel bored and purposeless, God can offer us a new chance to make a difference in our immediate world and in the world at large.

When we pray to God to renew our spirit and rekindle our inner flame, new opportunities appear and people come into our lives who are willing to support us in our goals and dreams. We are reborn into a new life of passion, purpose, and power. Broken places become whole. With God, we are made new again.

Lord, refresh my broken spirit tonight. Life has worn down the edges of my passion for living, and I am tired. Help me find a newfound sense of worth and wonder. Instill in me a sensation of seeing my life as if for the first time, in all its magic. Renew in me the desire to be a light of good in the world and to fulfill the destiny you gave me upon the moment of my birth. Your spirit is breath in my lungs and fire for my soul. Give me new wings upon which I can soar to the greatest of heights. Amen.

Blessed are you who are poor, for yours is the kingdom of God. Blessed are you who are hungry now, for you will be filled. Blessed are you who weep now, for you will laugh.
—Luke 6:20–21

Lord, please help me serve as an example for others who are hoping to renew their lives. I want them to look at me and know of your transformative powers. I want to show them how you, Heavenly Father, can take something dead and wasted in spirit and turn it into a living, thriving being, overflowing with love. You have worked miracles in my life, and I want to be a testament to your holy power. Mold me into your image, so I may encourage others in their journeys. Amen.

I am the gate. Whoever enters by me will be saved, and will come in and go out and find pasture. The thief comes only to steal and kill and destroy.
I came that they may have life,
and have it abundantly.
—John 10:9–10

*Dear God, for another day, for another minute, for
another chance to live and serve you, I am grateful.
Please keep me free... from fear of the future,
from anxiety about tomorrow,
from bitterness towards anyone,
from cowardice in the face of danger,
from laziness in my daily work,
from failure before opportunity,
from weakness when your power is at hand.
But fill me... With love that knows no bounds,
With sympathy that reaches all,
With courage that cannot be shaken,
With faith strong enough for the darkness,
With strength sufficient for my tasks,
With loyalty to your kingdom,
With wisdom to meet life's mysteries,
With power to lift me to yourself.
Be with me for another day and
use me as you will. Amen.*
—"The Daily Offering," from *The Pilgrim's Prayer Book*

God, make me whole again. I have been broken and splintered by the stresses of life and feel as though a huge hole has opened up inside me. It is like a void that only your grace and love can fill. Believe me, I have tried to fill it with so many things, and I come to you battered by my foolish attempts to find what only you can give me. Renew my body, mind, and spirit, so that I may see things through fresh eyes and face things with newfound energy and willingness. Thanks be to you, God, for making me whole again.

Blessed be the Lord, for he has heard the sound of my pleadings. The Lord is my strength and my shield; in him my heart trusts; so I am helped, and my heart exults, and with my song I give thanks to him.

—Psalm 28:6–7

Lord, I don't know when I've felt this completely drained. I know you can see what a state I'm in. I feel like I barely have enough energy to make it through the day. I'm so empty inside that I have nothing to give to the people I love. And they notice. Fill me, Lord, as only you can. Fill me with your purpose for me, that I may be full to overflowing—all to your glory!

~ ~

May the God of hope fill you with all joy and peace in believing, so that you may abound in hope by the power of the Holy Spirit.
—Romans 15:13

~ ~

Creator God, it's always so amazing to see the first signs of spring. The crocuses that pop up through the snow, the bright green buds on the trees, they all catch us by surprise because we've become so accustomed to the cold and dreary days. But you, O Lord, revive us with the beauty of your creation! How good it is for us to remember that just as you protect the seeds and plants under the winter snow and bring them back to life, you also protect us in the dreariest of times. Thank you for new life in our world and in our hearts, Lord!

❧ ❧

You came near when I called on you; you said, "Do not fear!" You have taken up my cause, O Lord, you have redeemed my life.
—Lamentations 3:57–58

❧ ❧

Lord, when I look at how far I have come in my spiritual journey, I am amazed. It is only through the continued presence of the Holy Spirit that I have been able to transform myself. When I look at how far I have to go, though, I am afraid. I don't know how I will ever be able to change the habits and release the thoughts that hold me back. But I have faith that if I continue to return to you, renewing myself in your Word, that I can make the changes I need in order to become the person you want me to be. Please be with me, guiding me along the way, giving me the strength for each new step as I grow in your love. I ask this in your name, Amen.

O sing to the Lord a new song; sing to the Lord, all the earth. Sing to the Lord, bless his name; tell of his salvation from day to day. Declare his glory among the nations, his marvelous works among all the peoples. For great is the Lord, and greatly to be praised; he is to be revered above all gods.

—Psalm 96:1–4

O Lord, how precious is the water that flows down from the mountains to restore our land after a long drought. Thank you for sending the fresh, life-giving water to nourish our lawns, our flowerbeds, and our bodies. Yet, as desirable as that water is, Lord, we know that the living water we receive from you is the most precious of all. Thank you, Lord, for sending your living water to refresh our parched souls. We stand in the rejuvenating stream of your love and grace.

Jesus answered her, "If you knew the gift of God, and who it is that is saying to you, 'Give me a drink,' you would have asked him, and he would have given you living water."
—John 4:10

Lord, in you I find renewal and the courage to see life in a different way. By following your will, I am filled with an excitement, energy, and enthusiasm for life that recharges my purpose and gives me new hope that all will be well. I thank you for this chance to do things differently, with a different perspective, and to follow the light you put out for me, making easier my path. In your presence I know I can accomplish anything and live my dreams. Amen.

Like obedient children, do not be conformed to the desires that you formerly had in ignorance. Instead, as he who called you is holy, be holy yourselves in all your conduct; for it is written, "You shall be holy, for I am holy."
—1 Peter 1:14–16

Lord, I know you created me and you don't make mistakes, but sometimes I think I need an extreme makeover! I'm not talking about the outward me this time, I'm talking about the inner me, the me that only I know. My heart, my attitudes, my feelings, even my thoughts about my family could use some refreshing, Lord. I give you permission to do some serious remodeling in this house called me. I trust you and only you to make me over, knowing you will also make me completely perfect someday.

Create in me a clean heart, O God,
and put a new and right spirit within me.
—Psalm 51:10

God, this marathon of life sometimes leaves my feet sore and aching. But with the grace of your everlasting love, I know that I will be given new strength to lift me up and carry me along when my feet just cannot go on. You have always been there for me, and I know that you will always be there for me now, even when it appears that I am on my own. All I need to do is look within and I will see that I have some-one running this marathon alongside me, offering a helping hand and an encouraging word when I think I cannot take one more step.

Heavenly Father, when I was baptized, I immediately became your child, dedicated to your purpose. But you remind us again and again that we must continue to renew ourselves and grow in relationship to you. Each day, then, be with me as I struggle to become more and more Christlike, letting go of past habits and becoming a living testament to you and your transformative powers. Amen.

Lord, some days I wonder what's happening to this body of mine. Aches and pains appear for no reason, and the wrinkles are so plentiful there's no use counting anymore! I know you look at inner beauty, not outward beauty, so I come to you to ask you to give me your perspective on this whole aging process. Am I as beautiful in your eyes as I was the day you made me? That's what I choose to believe, Lord, and that's all that really matters to me. Keep making me more beautiful on the inside, and I'll try to make friends with the person in the mirror.

＞＜ ＞＜

Jesus, one of my relationships is faltering, and we need your presence. I have faith that you can make all things new again, and you can revive even those things that seem to be beyond hope. I ask that you help us shed our old ways of acting and reacting, that we may make a new relationship, dedicated to and consecrated in you. With your help, we can heal past hurts and forge new ways of relating that will bring us closer to you, together and individually. Please be with us as we work on this challenge. Amen.

~ ~

Sometimes, God, I feel like a withered-up plant in desperate need of sunshine and water. Yet there seems to be neither in sight. Then I remember my source, and I turn to the warmth of your love, God, to be replenished and renewed and to open my heart to the sun again. Like rain, you quench my thirst and wash away my fears. Your loving light scatters the darkness I stumble about in. I feel like I can hold my head up high again, in the renewing grace of your presence in my life.

~ ~

*Restore to me the joy of your salvation,
and sustain in me a willing spirit.*
—Psalm 51:12

Lord, it seems as if so many marriages are in
need of renewal. I come to you today to ask
for your intervention in all marriages. Restore
husbands and wives to the positions of respect
and love you want them to have, Lord. Allow
them to see one another through your eyes and
to remember all the reasons they fell in love in
the first place. Reignite the fires of romance,
Lord! This world is hard on marriage, but you
created it for the people you love, and only
you can make it as rich and rewarding as you
intended it to be. Give us an abiding love for
one another, Lord. Teach us to cherish the
marriages you ordained. Amen.

Father in Heaven, I want to sing a new song so all can hear me. I want my lips to praise your name, to proclaim the rebirth of hope in Jesus Christ. I long to be a beacon for others and show them the path to new life through you! I offer myself to you, to be used for your purposes. Find my sacrifice pleasing in your sight. It is not much, but it is all I have to offer. I ask this in the name of your Son, Jesus Christ. Amen.

All the trees of the field shall know that I am the Lord. I bring low the high tree, I make high the low tree. I dry up the green tree and make the dry tree flourish.
—Ezekiel 17:24

Lord, they say the definition of insanity is doing the same thing over and over again and expecting different results. I often find myself running around in circles, exhausted and resigned to my fate. But you alone have the power to show me new ways of thinking, of doing, and of being in the world. You alone can guide me to new paths I never imagined, where opportunities await and obstacles are few and far between. Each time I turn to you, I am reminded that every day is a new day and a new chance to live life in a whole new way. Amen.

You were taught to put away your former way of life, your old self, corrupt and deluded by its lusts, and to be renewed in the spirit of your minds, and to clothe yourself with the new self, created according to the likeness of God in true righteousness and holiness.
—Ephesians 4:22–24

God, sometimes I feel like a stale loaf of bread, as if I am living the same day over and over. I feel tired and resigned to living half a life, just getting by. I pray you will light a fire within me and reignite in me the interests and passions I once had that made my life so unique and filled with delight. Rekindle my desire to be better each day, to not settle for less, and to lift my eyes upward to what is possible, not downward to what is impossible. Fill me with a newfound purpose, that I may become as new as freshly baked bread.

Dear Lord, you have come to save us and make us new again in Christ! When we are baptized in your name, we can cast off our old life, like removing a dirty, stained shirt. We emerge, renewed, cloaked in sparkling robes that shine more brightly than the sun. Our sins are washed away, and we are free from our past. Please remind me that I can have that renewal of spirit at any time, just by praying to you and accepting your forgiveness. I ask in your name, Amen.

✦ ✦

Blessed be the God and Father of our Lord Jesus Christ! By his great mercy he has given us a new birth into a living hope through the resurrection of Jesus Christ from the dead, and into an inheritance that is imperishable, undefiled, and unfading, kept in heaven for you, who are being protected by the power of God through faith for a salvation ready to be revealed in the last time.

—1 Peter 1:3–5

✦ ✦

After another night of mindless television, Lord, I lie in bed and try to erase the images and thoughts swirling through my head. Why do we fall into the trap of wasting time this way? When I think of all the wonderful books

I haven't read or the time I could have invested in people in my family instead of actors in sitcoms, I feel ashamed. Renew my mind, Lord. Fill it with thoughts of you, with images of eternal glory, and with your restoring words of Scripture. Watch over me as I sleep, Lord, and let me wake refreshed—with the knowledge that you can and will direct my mind in the ways you would have it go.

Do not be conformed to this world, but be transformed by the renewing of your minds, so that you may discern what is the will of God—what is good and acceptable and perfect.
—Romans 12:2

Today I will put my faith in the Lord and let his love fill me with light. I will walk lightly, talk lightly, and live lightly, letting all that is good be my guide. On newfound wings I will soar, and with newfound hope I will give of myself to anyone who needs my help today. The love of the Lord cleanses me, making me a bright reflection of his goodness. May the Lord continue to renew me and restore to me the glory he intends me to have. May I be the blessing he intended me to be to everyone I meet.

Lord, I don't know why I try so hard not to cry when doing so always releases the stress and sadness I'm holding on to. Why does it take a sentimental commercial or a glimpse of a new baby in the grocery store to start the tears flowing? For when I've cried all I can, Lord, that's when you come along to renew and restore me. Thank you, Lord, for the cleansing gift of tears.

God, you are like water when I am parched with a thirst nothing else can fill. I drink of your love, and I am reborn with life force, able to see everything in a different light, able to make better choices when issues arise. And we both know they always do. Life is not supposed to always be easy, but with your guidance, I know that when hard times come calling, I can find the energy and wisdom I need to get that extra burst of hope and faith. With you, God, nothing is impossible and all things are achievable.

⤚ ⤚

But those who wait for the Lord shall renew their strength, they shall mount up with wings like eagles, they shall run and not be weary, they shall walk and not faint.
—Isaiah 40:31

⤚ ⤚

Dear Lord, you have removed my transgressions in the blink of an eye. You grant me daily renewal in the name of your Son, Jesus Christ. You are with me always, in all things. Because I have committed myself to you, I don't need to wear the sins of my past upon me or carry my mistakes with me. I can lay them at your feet, starting anew each morning. Thank you for redeeming me and allowing me to follow you. Amen.

Barren is my heart tonight, Lord. I've been hurt and broken, and I feel like I can't go on. Worse still, I feel there is no point. I pray that you watch over me as I lay down to rest. While I sleep, fill me with hope and faith, just enough to get through one more day. For I know that if I can make it through one day, you will empower me again to make it through another. I pray that your strength will be mine and your courage will inspire me to face my problems with a renewed belief that with you at my side, I will come out stronger and better than ever. Come walk with me through this barren plain, and guide me to the valley of blessings that awaits over the horizon, just out of sight. Amen.

＊ ＊

Lord, as I grow older, I sense my body beginning to decline. Someday my eyes won't be as keen, my legs won't be as strong, and my energy will sometimes flag. But I welcome these outward changes. As the days pass and my physical body transforms, I rejoice, for I know my inner spirit is transforming as well. Someday I will release this temporary body, leaving it behind as I experience total renewal, joining you in everlasting joy. Thank you for making me one of your own. Amen.

＊ ＊

So we do not lose heart. Even though our outer nature is wasting away, our inner nature is being renewed day by day. For this slight momentary affliction is preparing us for an eternal weight of glory beyond all measure, because we look not at what can be seen but at what cannot be seen; for what can be seen is temporary, but what cannot be seen is eternal.
—2 Corinthians 4:16–18

God, when I could not walk another step, you lifted me up and we flew. When I could not get out of bed with illness, you restored me to health again. When I could not see the light at the end of the tunnel, you walked with me in the darkness until it appeared. When I could not find the solution to my problems, you filled my mind with fresh ideas and new ways of looking at things. To you I give thanks for always reviving my body, mind, and spirit when I feel I have nothing left to give. You are my rock and my sunlight, a place upon which to stand strong and a light to guide my way when I am ready to move forward again. Thank you, dear God.

⋆ ⋆

Today, Lord, I want to lift up to you all the mothers of young children. Their days can seem so long, Lord, and the expressions of appreciation for what they do can be so few and far between. Lord, renew them with the understanding that they are doing mighty and meaningful work. Smile down on them today, Lord, wherever they may be, and give them the encouragement and the confidence that only comes from you. Assure them that you see every shoe they tie, every spill they clean up, and every little tear they dry. Each time they hug their children, Lord, may they feel your arms around them. Thank you, Lord.

⋆ ⋆

Lord, you sent your Son to us not to make our old lives better, but to give us entirely new lives in Christ. Help me to cast off all my old ways of living and being so I can become something completely new and different, with your help. I don't want to improve; I want to be reborn in Christ. I pray for the miracle of your love to change me, making me unrecognizable and completely, utterly yours. I ask in your name, Amen.

Listen, I will tell you a mystery! We will not all die, but we will all be changed, in a moment, in the twinkling of an eye, at the last trumpet. For the trumpet will sound, and the dead will be raised imperishable, and we will be changed.
—1 Corinthians 15:51–52

Heavenly Father, I am tired of the struggle. Every inch I make in the battle against sin takes all my energy, and I am sapped dry. No matter where I turn, I feel like I must be constantly on my guard. I need the renewal of spirit that only you can bring. Please help me. Be with me. Give me strength and allow me to rest, so I may continue to do your good works and fight for your kingdom on earth. Amen.

Though the fig tree does not blossom, and no fruit is on the vines; though the produce of the olive fails and the fields yield no food; though the flock is cut off from the fold and there is no herd in the stalls, yet I will rejoice in the Lord; I will exult in the God of my salvation. God, the Lord, is my strength; he makes my feet like the feet of a deer, and makes me tread upon the heights.
—Habakkuk 3:17–19

Thank you for going with me on my walk today, Lord. You know how exhausted I was when I started out. But the longer I walked, the more things I thought about to bring to you in prayer, the more aware I became of your awesome creation all around me, and the more rejuvenated I became. Sending those three deer into my path was an especially nice touch! You are the bounce in my step, Lord. Thanks for the walk.

Dear Heavenly Father, you are a God of paradox. You brought your Son, our Savior, to us in the form of a baby. You announced his coming first to the poorest of shepherds. And you have told us that it is the weak and humble, not the rich and proud, who will inherit the earth. It is no surprise then that in order to have everlasting life, we must first die. Just as Jesus died on the cross and was raised to live again, we also will receive eternal life after death. I pray that you will remind me that much of what is true is beyond my limited understanding. Help me trust in you and have faith that with you even the impossible is possible. Amen.

Today, Lord, I just want to praise you for music! For its healing powers, its ability to lift us out of the doldrums, and its ability to restore a sense of hope and peace in us. When I hear the old hymns, I'm transported to the church of my childhood and can almost feel my mother's hand in mine again. When a contemporary praise song comes on my car radio, I just want to lift my hands through the sunroof and praise you all day long! Through music, I am elevated to a higher place, Lord—a place closer to you. And for that I am so grateful.